Instant Creating Data Models with PowerPivot How-to

Build better business intelligence with this practical guide to creating Excel data models with PowerPivot

Leo Taehyung Lee

BIRMINGHAM - MUMBAI

Instant Creating Data Models with PowerPivot How-to

First published: April 2013

Production Reference: 1180413

Published by Packt Publishing Ltd.
Livery Place
35 Livery Street
Birmingham B3 2PB, UK.

ISBN 978-1-84968-956-4

www.packtpub.com

Credits

Author
Leo Taehyung Lee

Reviewer
Mohammed Raza Saghar

Acquisition Editor
Andrew Duckworth

Commissioning Editor
Neha Nagwekar

Technical Editor
Hardik B. Soni

Project Coordinator
Joel Goveya

Proofreader
Jonathan Todd

Production Coordinators
Melwyn D'sa

Nilesh R. Mohite

Cover Work
Melwyn D'sa

About the Author

Leo Taehyung Lee is an outgoing individual with a diverse background and experiences. His studies in engineering along with the pursuit of a career in finance helped him work in various positions across diverse fields from R&D to patents as well as financial risk management. He has over 3 years of extensive experience in Excel, VBA, and is a Microsoft Certified Excel Expert in Excel 2010.

This book would not have been possible without the constant support from YN. Special thanks to YW for the encouragement and help in developing relevant skills.

About the Reviewer

Mohammed Raza Saghar is a Microsoft Certified Office 2007 and 2010 Master and a Microsoft Certified Excel Expert in 2003, 2007, and 2010 versions. He has Excel and VBA experience of more than 13 years and overall training experience of more than 3 years that also includes complete training of 48 batches at AFCKS Technologies (Pune, India) and 3 corporate trainings at a management college. Students like his training style, in-depth course coverage, approachability, and professionalism.

www.PacktPub.com

Support files, eBooks, discount offers and more

You might want to visit www.PacktPub.com for support files and downloads related to your book.

Did you know that Packt offers eBook versions of every book published, with PDF and ePub files available? You can upgrade to the eBook version at www.PacktPub.com and as a print book customer, you are entitled to a discount on the eBook copy. Get in touch with us at service@packtpub.com for more details.

At www.PacktPub.com, you can also read a collection of free technical articles, sign up for a range of free newsletters and receive exclusive discounts and offers on Packt books and eBooks.

http://PacktLib.PacktPub.com

Do you need instant solutions to your IT questions? PacktLib is Packt's online digital book library. Here, you can access, read and search across Packt's entire library of books.

Why Subscribe?

- ▸ Fully searchable across every book published by Packt
- ▸ Copy and paste, print and bookmark content
- ▸ On demand and accessible via web browser

Free Access for Packt account holders

If you have an account with Packt at www.PacktPub.com, you can use this to access PacktLib today and view nine entirely free books. Simply use your login credentials for immediate access.

Table of Contents

Preface

Microsoft PowerPivot is a free add-in for Excel, designed to allow the user to perform extensive data analysis while still working in a familiar environment. It allows the user to draw data from multiple sources, to build relationships between these data, to create custom data, and to work with hundreds of millions of rows. Through its step-by-step interactive tutorials, the user will become familiar with functionalities of PowerPivot, helping to make intelligent business analysis!

What this book covers

Installation (Simple) covers the installation of PowerPivot on Excel, as well as the installation of a sample database for future tutorials.

Importing data from the database (Advanced) helps you with downloading data from the sample database, the most common form that a data is stored in any business. The user will become familiar enough in obtaining relevant data that they may need for further usage.

Importing data from other files (Simple) deals with the fact that aside from a database, there are plenty of files available online or being used in a business. The tutorials in this recipe prepare and import many different types of data for future use.

Filtering data to be imported (Intermediate) covers importing data from the database and automatically storing it in PowerPivot for future usage. However, not all data are relevant nor useful and can easily be distinguished. The tutorial in this section will practice how to filter data when importing.

Creating a pivot table (Simple) helps you understand the data that we imported will be just that – raw data. The tutorial in this section will explore the pivot table to make the most sense out of the data.

Creating a pivot chart (Simple) deals with the fact that while pivot tables are nice, numbers are not as obvious as graphs and charts. Pivot charts and its features add a layer of analysis to the data at hand.

Managing data relationships (Simple) covers the fact that pulling data from many sources may cause confusion to a computer where it does not recognize how the data are related, even though it may be obvious to the user. This is where data relationships should be set up in order for Excel to recognize the data relationships properly.

Adding new custom columns (Intermediate) deals with the fact that in many occasions, raw data is very limited in sorting, arranging, and calculating data. Adding new custom columns of data is an easy way to address it using formulas similar to Excel.

Making data look presentable (Simple) covers the fact that, once finalized, pivot tables and pivot charts may be logical to an insider, but the true strength of business intelligence analysis lies in having anyone to be able to look at the results and make sense of them. This requires making data look presentable.

Publishing as Excel (Simple) covers the fact that Excel is the most common business software globally, so the best way to show the results of the analysis is to send the file directly—with some adjustments of course.

What you need for this book

In order to perform the interactive tutorials presented in this book, an instance of Microsoft Office Excel 2010 or better and an Internet connection are required. Other files may be downloaded from Internet sources as needed.

Who this book is for

An introductory book on PowerPivot for Excel for basic Excel users from students to non-IT personnel as well as small-business owners, who handle lots of data and are willing to go beyond the limitations of Excel without the need to learn a new language from scratch.

Conventions

In this book, you will find a number of styles of text that distinguish between different kinds of information. Here are some examples of these styles, and an explanation of their meaning.

Code words in text, folder names, filenames, file extensions, pathnames, dummy URLs, user input, and Twitter handles are shown as follows: "Copy the sheet `DeliveryTime01` and rename as `DeliveryTime02`."

A block of code is set as follows:

```
=year([OrderDate])
=month([OrderDate])
=if(or([Month]<3, [Month]=12), "Winter", if([Month]<6, "Spring",
if([Month]<9, "Summer", "Fall")))
```

New terms and **important words** are shown in bold. Words that you see on the screen, in menus or dialog boxes for example, appear in the text like this: "Click on the **PivotTable** button near the middle of the top row and save as **New Worksheet**."

Reader feedback

Feedback from our readers is always welcome. Let us know what you think about this book—what you liked or may have disliked. Reader feedback is important for us to develop titles that you really get the most out of.

To send us general feedback, simply send an e-mail to `feedback@packtpub.com`, and mention the book title via the subject of your message.

If there is a topic that you have expertise in and you are interested in either writing or contributing to a book, see our author guide on `www.packtpub.com/authors`.

Customer support

Now that you are the proud owner of a Packt book, we have a number of things to help you to get the most from your purchase.

Downloading the sample files

You can download the sample files for all Packt books you have purchased from your account at `http://www.packtpub.com`. If you purchased this book elsewhere, you can visit `http://www.packtpub.com/support` and register to have the files e-mailed directly to you.

Errata

Although we have taken every care to ensure the accuracy of our content, mistakes do happen. If you find a mistake in one of our books—maybe a mistake in the text or the code—we would be grateful if you would report this to us. By doing so, you can save other readers from frustration and help us improve subsequent versions of this book. If you find any errata, please report them by visiting `http://www.packtpub.com/submit-errata`, selecting your book, clicking on the **errata submission form** link, and entering the details of your errata. Once your errata are verified, your submission will be accepted and the errata will be uploaded on our website, or added to any list of existing errata, under the Errata section of that title. Any existing errata can be viewed by selecting your title from `http://www.packtpub.com/support`.

Piracy

Piracy of copyright material on the Internet is an ongoing problem across all media. At Packt, we take the protection of our copyright and licenses very seriously. If you come across any illegal copies of our works, in any form, on the Internet, please provide us with the location address or website name immediately so that we can pursue a remedy.

Please contact us at `copyright@packtpub.com` with a link to the suspected pirated material.

We appreciate your help in protecting our authors, and our ability to bring you valuable content.

Questions

You can contact us at `questions@packtpub.com` if you are having a problem with any aspect of the book, and we will do our best to address it.

Instant Creating Data Models with PowerPivot How-to

Welcome to *Instant Creating Data Models with PowerPivot How-to* book. Whether the user is a small-business owner or an Excel pro, the features of PowerPivot will provide a strong business analytics tool that can help the user review past performance, identify trends, and predict future conditions. This book will guide the user in using all functionalities of Microsoft PowerPivot for Excel—from the installation steps for Excel 2010 to creating pivot tables and charts by setting up custom data and data relationships. So, let's get started!

Installation (Simple)

To get started with PowerPivot, you first need to install or enable it depending upon the version of Excel you are using. Not all versions of Excel may support PowerPivot. The majority of the functionality of PowerPivot mentioned in this book have been included in the new Excel 2013, such as managing data relationships. However, PowerPivot now comes as an add-in that must be enabled in Excel 2013 to fully utilize its capabilities such as writing custom data using **Data Analysis Expressions** (**DAX**) formula. For more information, please refer to *What's new in PowerPivot in Excel 2013* at http://office.microsoft.com/en-001/excel-help/whats-new-in-powerpivot-in-excel-2013-HA102893837.aspx.

This task will detail the steps required for installing PowerPivot in Excel 2010.

Getting ready

Microsoft PowerPivot for Excel requires Excel 2010 or above. Earlier versions of Excel, such as 2007, are not compatible with PowerPivot. Please ensure that Excel 2010 is installed properly.

How to do it...

1. Click on the **Download PowerPivot** button on the main page of `http://www.PowerPivot.com`.

2. Click on the **Instructions** link on the left-hand side of the page under the **Quick Links** tab. Follow the instructions to install .NET Framework 4.0 and Visual Studio 2010 Tools for Office Runtime.

3. Go to the top of the page and download the PowerPivot for Excel accordingly. x86 should be installed if the Excel is 32-bit, and x64 should be installed for a 64-bit Excel. The version of Excel 2010 can be checked by checking the **About Microsoft Excel** section under the **File | Help** menu as seen in the following screenshot:

4. After the installation is completed, the features of PowerPivot will be accessible under the new **PowerPivot** ribbon as highlighted in the following screenshot:

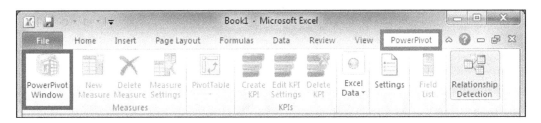

5. Ensure that it operates properly by clicking on the **PowerPivot Window** button as highlighted in the previous screenshot. It will open up a new window where we can import, organize, analyze, and publish data from various sources as shown in the following screenshot. This is the tool that we will be using throughout all the tasks.

6. Now we are fully equipped to use the Microsoft PowerPivot add-in for Excel 2010 – the business intelligence tool.

How it works...

The PowerPivot (http://www.powerpivot.com/) link will redirect you to the official Microsoft page where we can download the PowerPivot add-in for Excel. The installation of PowerPivot requires two programs to install properly (.NET Framework 4.0 and Visual Studio 2010 Tools for Office Runtime). We should download these two programs before we proceed with the download. The operating system has two types: 32-bit (x86) and 64-bit (x64). Downloading the appropriate version will enable PowerPivot to perform at its best in accessing and calculating the data.

PowerPivot is easy to use. It integrates itself with Excel, appearing as if it is the built-in property of Excel, and shares many of the same features as Excel, which makes our life easier. The new tab requires us to restart Excel to be seen. The actual data import, calculations, and other items are performed all within this external window. This window is PowerPivot, which supports millions of rows of data, faster calculations, and other features.

There's more...

It is important to install the correct bit version of PowerPivot. The 64-bit Excel and 64-bit PowerPivot will enable the computer to store, access, and calculate more items at once, which is a key feature in PowerPivot that allows users to analyze data greater than one million rows—something that regular Excel 2010 cannot do.

Importing data from the database (Advanced)

A database is an effective method to store and use data for large businesses, but its structure is very different from anything else. We will install a sample database and use its data throughout the rest of the book. If you are well aware of a database or do not plan on using a database at all, then this section is optional.

Getting ready

Before importing data from the database, we need to install the database client and the sample data itself. Then, we will import large amount of data from a database into PowerPivot. Please ensure that you have administrative rights to install on your computer.

How to do it...

1. Download and install the small version of Microsoft SQL Server 2008 R2 SP2 – Express with Tools (`SQLEXPRWT_x64_ENU.exe` or `SQLEXPRWT_x86_ENU.exe`), which is sufficient for our purpose. It can be downloaded from `http://www.microsoft.com/en-ca/download/details.aspx?id=30438`.

2. Download the sample database **AdventureWorks** by selecting **AdventureWorks2008R2 Data File** at `http://msftdbprodsamples.codeplex.com/releases/view/59211`.

3. Open SQL Server Management Studio as an administrator. Click on **Attach...** as shown in the following screenshot:

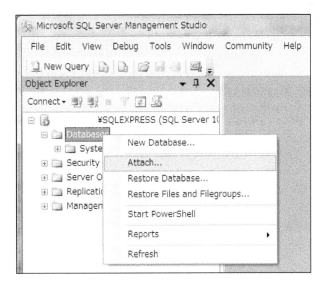

4. In the next screen, select **Log** in the **database details** section and click on **Remove** as shown in the following screenshot. This will remove the logs. Now you can press the **OK** button.

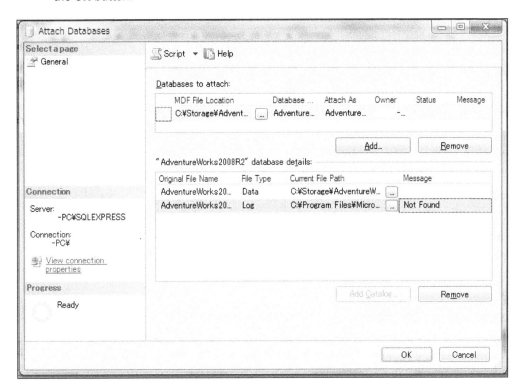

5. Once the sample database has successfully been installed, it will be visible on the left-hand side pane of the SQL Server Management Studio. After confirming, open Excel 2010 with PowerPivot.

6. In Excel 2010, open up the PowerPivot window. Select **From Database | From SQL Server**. Select the details as shown in the following screenshot. If the server name is not available, type in `PC-NAME\SQLEXPRESS`.

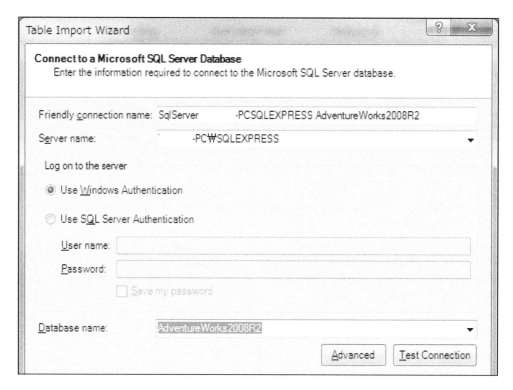

7. Then, select 13 tables with **Person** in the **Schema** column and click on **Finish**. It will import the tables into PowerPivot.

Congratulations! You have successfully imported tens of thousands of rows from the database in just a few seconds. Browse through a few sheets and confirm that we have successfully imported data from SQL database, and then save it as an Excel file named `DatabaseData.xlsx` and close. It should be roughly a 16 MB file.

How it works...

Through the installation of SQL database and the sample database, a database with sample data was created on your personal computer. Then, we have simply accessed and imported all data into PowerPivot for Excel. If the data is updated in the database, we can get the latest data simply by refreshing PowerPivot as the data are linked.

The data may not make much sense at the moment if the user is unfamiliar with the database structure, but it will make more sense in later recipes.

There's more...

If you have problems attaching a database, it is most likely an access error. Try to move the AdventureWorks file to another location, and ensure that SQL Server Management Studio was opened as an administrator.

The PowerPivot data that was imported from the database can be updated by simply pressing the **Refresh** button, just a few buttons to the right of the **From Database** button.

Excel 2013

PowerPivot is a built-in add-in for Excel 2013. To enable, please refer to `http://office.` `microsoft.com/en-001/excel-help/start-powerpivot-in-excel-2013-add-` `in-HA102837097.aspx` for instructions on how to enable the PowerPivot add-in.

Importing data from other files (Simple)

PowerPivot has the ability to aggregate and connect data from multiple sources. We will import some data from the Web into PowerPivot, which we may use later on in conjunction with the data imported from the database.

How to do it...

1. The web page `http://data.worldbank.org/indicator/NY.GDP.PCAP.` `PP.CD` contains historical GDP for each nation in the world, which can be simply downloaded as an Excel file. Open up the new Excel file using PowerPivot as shown in the following screenshot:

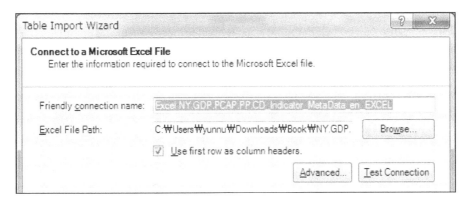

2. Select both the tables, and check the resulting sheet. Save as GDPData.xlsx for later usage.

3. Similarly, download the unemployment rate data as an XLS (Excel) file from http://www.oecd-ilibrary.org/employment/employment-and-labour-markets-key-tables-from-oecd_20752342, which contains the historical unemployment rate of each OECD nation. This will not import to PowerPivot directly as the file is in the .xls format, but is based on another format (XML). Open it in Excel and save as a CSV file.

4. Use PowerPivot to import the CSV file and save as UnemploymentData.csv.

Downloading the sample files

You can download the sample files for all Packt books you have purchased from your account at http://www.packtpub.com. If you purchased this book elsewhere, you can visit http://www.packtpub.com/support and register to have the files e-mailed directly to you.

How it works...

PowerPivot has a built-in convertor that converts the data from various sources into PowerPivot data. These results can be saved separately as we have just performed and can be aggregated together at a later stage.

Similar to the data from the database, the changes made to the source files (that is, Excel files) may be updated in the PowerPivot file by simply clicking the **Refresh** button.

There's more...

PowerPivot has limited support for certain sets of files, but these are more than enough for regular analysis.

Despite the fact that PowerPivot contains a tool called **Importing from Text** for the .txt and .csv files, and that we have manually created and used a .csv file, these files are not readily used anymore as most institutions now use Excel in providing data.

Filtering the data to be imported (Intermediate)

PowerPivot stores all the data that it imported from other sources. Despite the fact that PowerPivot is able to handle millions of rows of data (based on memory availability), it is always more efficient and effective to only import the relevant data. We will re-import data from the database and from Excel, and filter the data in the process.

Getting ready

In order to filter data, it is necessary for us to understand which data is relevant and which is not. The term "more the merrier" does not apply in this case, as we will only use these filtered data that are relevant throughout this book.

How to do it...

Reproduce the steps for importing data from the database as follows:

1. In Excel 2010, open up the PowerPivot window. Select **From Database | From SQL Server**. Select the details as shown in the following screenshot. If the server name is not available, then type in PC-NAME\SQLEXPRESS.

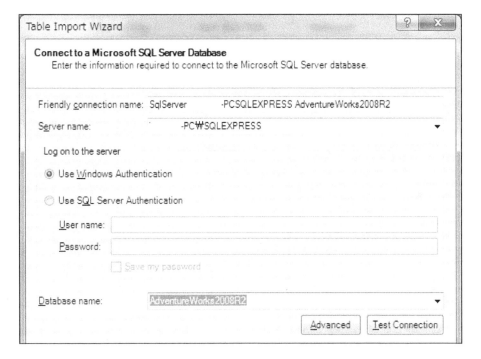

2. However, this time, click the **Preview & Filter** button as highlighted in the following screenshot for each of the 13 tables.

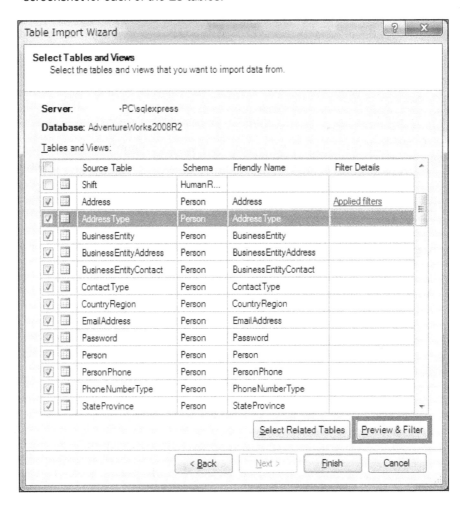

3. It will display a preview of every table that we are importing—and we haven't explored what each column means. However, one easy thing is to remove logs and other items that may be necessary for the database, but not for us. This may include logs, last modified date, last user modified, and so on. For the first table **Address**, deselect the last two columns **rowguid** and **ModifiedDate** as shown in the following screenshot:

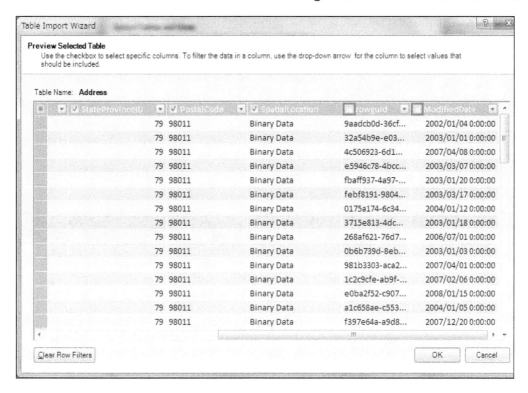

4. After deselecting, click on **OK** and we will see that new comment, **Applied filters**, will appear for the table under the column **Filter Details**, as shown in the screenshot in step 2. Repeat this procedure for every table, deselecting the data that we are sure will not be useful. Save the final datafile as `DatabaseData_v2.xlsx`. The file should be about 5 MB, around 11 to 12 MB smaller than the original one.

5. Similarly, repeat the step for the GDP datafile by deselecting the columns from 1970 to 1999. Import and then save the final data as `GDPData_v2.xlsx`. This filtered data should be about 375 KB, less than half of the size of the original file that would be 848 KB.

How it works...

Before, even though we only selected 13 tables out of the whole database, each table still contained unnecessary items such as logs. Depending on how large the database is, the amount of logs may be very large and space-consuming, and by simply filtering out those logs and/or other irrelevant data, we are able to work more efficiently and effectively with the correct sets of data. PowerPivot allows this by enabling the user to filter the data during the importation process by unchecking the unnecessary columns, so that only the necessary columns that were checked are imported, as we have previously practiced.

By simply comparing the file size, it is evident that filtering data becomes more necessary as the amount of data for analysis becomes larger. The data that we imported from the database is much less than hundreds of thousands of rows, but we already managed to save about 35 percent of the file size (and the corresponding calculation time) by unchecking non-significant columns during the import stage.

There's more...

As we become more familiar and proficient with data, we can even become more selective, selecting only the most relevant tables with the necessary columns. However, it requires a complete understanding of the database structure.

Creating a pivot table (Simple)

A pivot table is the core business intelligence tool that helps to turn meaningless data from various sources to a meaningful result. By using different ways of presenting data, we are able to identify relations between seemingly separate data and reach conclusions to help us identify our strengths and areas of improvement.

In this section, we will use the data prepared in previous recipes to make some pivot tables that can help us make smart business decisions!

Getting ready

Prepare the two files entitled `DatabaseData_v2.xlsx` and `GDPData_v2.xlsx` from the previous recipes. We will be using these results along with other data sources to create a meaningful PowerPivot table that will be used for intelligent business analysis.

How to do it...

For each of the two files prepared in the previous recipes, we will build upon the file and add a pivot table to it, gaining exposure using the data we are already familiar with.

The following are the steps to create a pivot table with the `DatabaseData_v2.xlsx` file, which results in the creation of a `DatabaseData_v3.xlsx` file:

1. Open the PowerPivot window of the `DatabaseData_v2.xlsx` file with its 13 tables.
2. Click on the **PivotTable** button near the middle of the top row and save as **New Worksheet**.
3. Select the checkboxes as shown in the following screenshot:
   - Select **CountryRegion | Name** and move it under **Row Labels**
   - Select **Address | City** and move it under **Row Labels**

   □ Select **Address | AddressLine1** as **Count of AddressLine1** and move it under **Values**

4. Now, this shows the number of clients per city and per country. However, it is very difficult to navigate, as each country name has to be collapsed in order to see the next country.

5. Let us move the **CountryRegion | Name** column to **Slicers Vertical**. Now, the **PowerPivot Field List** dashboard should appear as shown in the following screenshot:

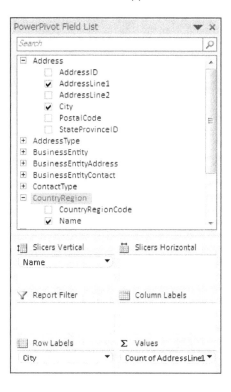

6. Now, the pivot table should display simple results: the number of clients in a region, filterable by the country using slicers.

7. Let us apply some formatting to allow for a better understanding of the data.

8. Right-click on **Name** under the **Slicers Vertical** area of the **PowerPivot Field List** dashboard. Select **Field Settings**, then change the name to `Country Name`. We now see that the title of the slicer has changed from **Name** to **Country Name**, allowing anyone who views this data to understand better what the data represents.

9. Similarly, right-click on **Count of AddressLine1** under **Values**, select **Edit Measure**, and then change its name to `Number of Clients`. Also change the data title **City** under the **Row Labels** area to `City Name`. The result should appear as shown in the following screenshot:

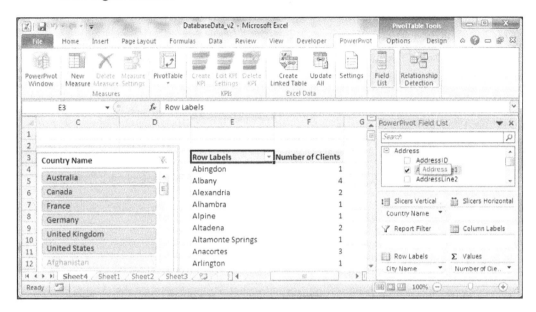

10. Let's see our results change as we click on different country names. We can filter for multiple countries by holding the *Ctrl* key while clicking, and can remove all filters by clicking the small button on the top-right of slicers. This is definitely easier to navigate through and to understand compared to what we did at first without using slicers, which is how it would appear in Excel 2010 without PowerPivot.

11. However, this table is still too big. Clicking on **Canada** gives too many cities whose names many of us have not heard about before. Let us break the data further down by including states/provinces.

12. Select **StateProvince | Name** and move it under **Slicers Horizontal** and change its title to `State Name`. It is a good thing that we are renaming these as we go along. Otherwise, there would have been two datasets called **Name**, and anyone would be confused as we moved along.

13. Now, we should see the state names filter on the top, the country name filter on the left, and a list of cities with the number of clients in the middle part. This, however, is kind of awkward. Let us rearrange the filters by having the largest filter (country) at the top and the sub-filter. (state) on the left-hand side This can be done simply by dragging the **Country Name** dataset to **Slicers Horizontal** and **State Name** to **Slicers Vertical**. After moving the slicers around a bit, the result should appear as shown in the following screenshot:

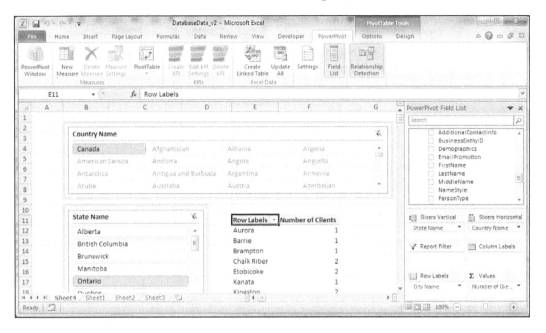

14. Again, play with the results and try to understand the features: try filtering by a country—and by a state/province—now there are limited numbers of cities shown for each country and each state/province, making it easier to see the list of cities.

15. However, for countries such as the United States, there are just too many states. Let us change the formatting of the vertical filter to display three states per line, so it is easier to find the state we are looking for. This can be done by right-clicking on the vertical filter, selecting **Size and Properties | Position and Layout**, and then by changing the **Number of Columns** value.

16. Repeat the same step for **Country Name** to display six columns and then change the sizes of the filters to look more selectable. Change the name of the sheet as PivotTable and then save the file as DatabaseData_v3.xlsx.

The following are the steps to create a pivot table with the GDPData_v2.xlsx file, which results in the creation of a GDPData_v3.xlsx file:

1. Open the PowerPivot window of the GDPData_v2.xlsx file with its two tables.

2. Click on the **PivotTable** button near the middle of the top row and save as **New Worksheet**.

3. Move the dataset from the year 2000 to the year 2010 to the **Value** field, and move **Country Name** in the **Row Labels** field, and **Country Name** again into the **Slicers Horizontal** field. In the slicer, select five countries: **Canada**, **China**, **Korea**, **Japan**, and **United States** as shown in the following screenshot:

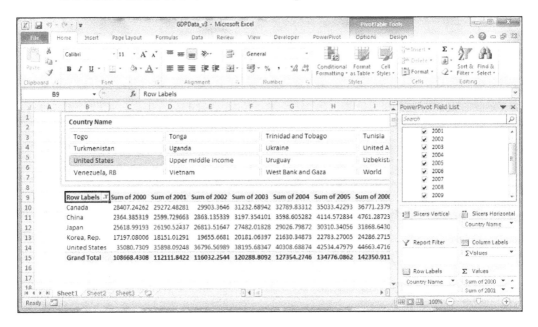

4. Select all fields and reduce the number of its decimal places. We can now clearly see that GDP in China has tripled over the decade, and that only China and Korea saw an increase in GDP from 2008 to 2009 while the GDP of other nations dropped due to the 2008 financial crisis.

5. Knowing the relevant background information of world finance events, we can make intelligent analysis such as which markets to invest in if we are worried about another financial crisis taking place.

6. As the data get larger in size, looking at the GDP number becomes increasingly difficult. In such cases, we can switch the type of data displayed by using available buttons in the **PivotTable Tools | Options** menu, the **Show Value As** button. Play around with it and see how it works: **% of Column Total** shows each GDP as a percentage of the year, while **% Different From** allows the user to set one value as the standard and compare the rest to it, and the **Rank Largest to Smallest** option simply shows the ranking based on which country earns the most GDP.

7. Change the name of the sheet as `PivotTable` and then save the file as `GDPData_v3.xlsx`.

How it works...

We looked at two different files and focused on two different fields. The first file was more qualitative and showed the relationship between regions and number of clients, using various features of pivot tables such as slicers. We also looked at how to format various aspects of a pivot table for easier processing and for a better understanding of the represented data.

Slicers embedded in the pivot table are a unique and very powerful feature of PowerPivot that allow us to sort through data simply by clicking the different criteria. The increasing numbers of slicers help to customize the data further, enabling the user to create all sorts of data imaginable. There are no differences in horizontal and vertical slicers aside from the fact that they are at different locations.

From the second file, we focused more on the quantitative data and different ways of representing the data. By using slicers to limit the number of countries, we were able to focus more on the data presented, and manage to represent the GDP in various formats such as percentages and ranks, and were able to compare the difference between the numbers by selecting one as a standard.

A similar method of representing data in a different format could be applied to the first file to show the percentage of clients per nation, and so on.

There's more...

We covered the very basic setup of creating a pivot table. In future recipes, we will analyze creating relationships between data and creating custom fields, so that better results are created. So don't worry about why the pivot table looks so small!

For those who do not like working with a pivot table, there is also a feature that will convert all cells into Excel formula. Under the **PowerPivot Tools** | **OLAP Tools** option, the **Convert to Formula** button does exactly that. However, be warned that it cannot be undone as the changes are permanent.

Creating a pivot chart (Simple)

With small amounts of data, the pivot table is sufficient for most types of data. However, as the data get larger, it is much easier to represent the data using graphical methods such as lines, pies, and bars. The good news for us is that creating a pivot chart from a pivot table is very simple, and it is very easy to change and update fields as needed. We will make a number of different charts for the pivot tables created in the previous recipes.

Getting ready

To proceed with creating pivot charts, we need the source data first. Luckily for us, that would be the pivot tables created in the previous recipe.

How to do it...

As usual, we will build upon files from previous recipes and add the pivot chart so that we may see where the data comes from and why it is significant.

The following are the steps to create a pivot chart with the `DatabaseData_v3.xlsx` file, which results in the creation of the `PivotChart` sheet in it:

1. Open the `DatabaseData_v3.xlsx` file again. Open the PowerPivot window and click on **PivotChart** (instead of the **PivotTable** button), located as a drop-down menu of the **PivotTable** button. Save it as **New Worksheet**.

    □   Select **CountryRegion | Name** and move it under **Slicers Vertical**

    □   Select **StateProvince | Name** and move it under **Slicers Vertical**

    □   Select **Address | City** and move it under **Slicers Vertical**

    □   Select **BusinessEntityAddress | BusinessEntityID** as **Count of BusinessEntityID** and move it under **Values**

2. Then, rename each field accordingly (`Country Name`, `State Name`, and `City Name`), copy the highlighted chart, and paste it below as shown in the following screenshot:

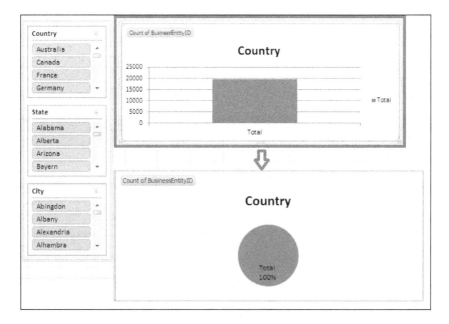

3. Change the chart type of the bottom chart to a pie chart.

4. From here, there are three different types of reports that we can easily create.

5. Place **CountryRegion | Name** under the **Axis Fields** area, and now we have a chart of number of clients per country, represented both as a bar graph and as a pie graph as shown in the following screenshot:

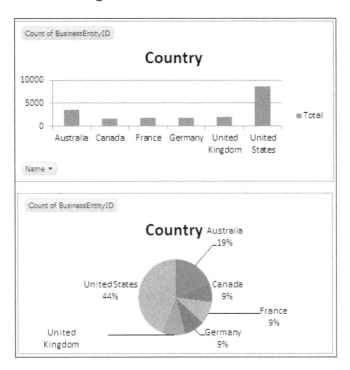

6. Similar steps can be repeated for state/province and for city. Of course, because it will list all states for all the countries, the charts will be very disorganized. Play around with it and filter it to select only one country. For instance, Germany will appear as shown in the following screenshot:

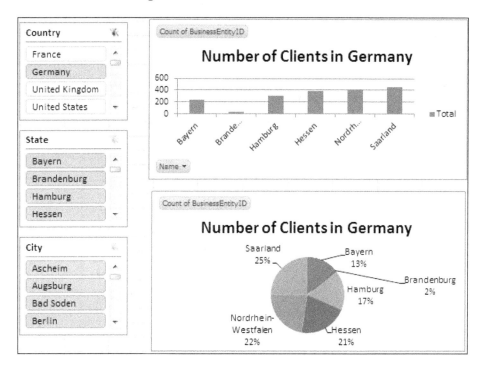

7. Once we are finished with changing chart types, filters, and other ways to create charts to represent the data, rename the sheet as `PivotChart` and save it and close.

8. Certain chart types are more effective than others in representing a specific type of data. We have created a chart from the beginning here, adding and removing datasets just like the pivot table.

The following are the steps to create a pivot chart with the GDPData_v3.xlsx file:

1. Open the GDPData_v3.xlsx file again. Click on the pivot table.

2. Under the **PowerPivot Tools | PivotChart** option select a chart type. We will create a column chart first, then copy the chart, and change the second chart type to **Doughnut**. Change the doughnut's chart layout to **Layout 3** and the result will be as shown in the following screenshot:

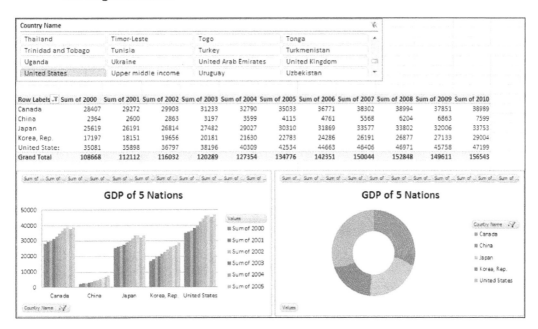

3. The column chart shows the generally increasing GDP per nation, but the numbers for China are very small and hard to compare. The doughnut chart is more effective in showing the exponentially increasing GDP of China, but is still difficult.

4. For each of the **Sum of …** column, change the **Show Value As** button as **% of…** with **China** as its base. This will display all other GDP as a percentage of China. The resulting bar graph shows that the GDP of China showed great growth year after year compared to other countries. It would appear as follows:

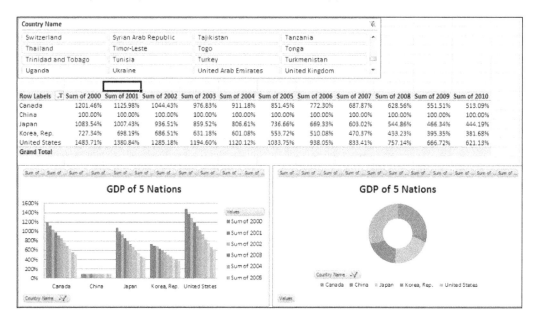

Row Labels	Sum of 2000	Sum of 2001	Sum of 2002	Sum of 2003	Sum of 2004	Sum of 2005	Sum of 2006	Sum of 2007	Sum of 2008	Sum of 2009	Sum of 2010
Canada	1201.46%	1125.98%	1044.43%	976.83%	911.18%	851.45%	772.30%	687.87%	628.56%	551.51%	513.09%
China	100.00%	100.00%	100.00%	100.00%	100.00%	100.00%	100.00%	100.00%	100.00%	100.00%	100.00%
Japan	1083.54%	1007.43%	936.51%	859.52%	806.61%	736.66%	669.33%	603.02%	544.86%	466.34%	444.19%
Korea, Rep.	727.34%	698.19%	686.51%	631.18%	601.08%	553.72%	510.08%	470.37%	433.23%	395.35%	381.68%
United States	1483.71%	1380.84%	1285.18%	1194.60%	1120.12%	1033.75%	938.05%	833.41%	757.14%	666.72%	621.13%
Grand Total											

How it works...

We explored both ways of creating a pivot chart: from the PowerPivot window directly, and directly from the pivot table. Pivot charts, as evidenced, are very simple to create in the same fashion as the pivot table, but with a greater range of options for displaying the data in a meaningful manner.

The more qualitative data (`DatabaseData.xslx`) were focused on counting the numbers by the country, by the state, and by the city. This was achieved by setting one axis as one of these and filtering correspondingly. In our case, the pie graph was the most appropriate in showing the percentage of number of clients per region, allowing the user to make an intelligent business decision to focus marketing on other regions with less number of clients.

In the more quantitative data (`GDPData.xslx`), we focused more on the comparison between different variables over the years. China has shown strong growth, and Korea has got-along through the 2008 financial crisis due to its less financial-focused and more industrial-focused economy, which helps the user make an intelligent business decision to invest or not invest in different nations based on their growth and their resilience to a global financial crisis.

In addition, as seen in the GDP data, changes in the ways of representing data (percentage, and so on) are reflected in the corresponding pivot table charts. The combined representation of data using both a pivot table and a pivot chart enables the user to identify trends in percentage levels as well as on absolute levels.

There's more...

As an additional item, try switching the rows and columns by pressing the **Switch Row/Column** button under the **PivotChart Tools | Design** tab. This will put the years as rows and countries as columns, which shows an interesting difference in how the chart appears.

Also, if we need two different types of chart on the same page, we can simply create two separate pivot tables and charts, and then move the charts together onto another sheet to represent different sets of data, which refers to a similar set of data.

Managing data relationships (Simple)

In previous recipes, the data relationships were auto-generated by PowerPivot. This relationship in PowerPivot is similar to how a database manages data from various tables using keys. We will practice building relationships to reproduce our data and incorporate different types of data together.

How to do it...

As the tables contain different types of data, PowerPivot may not comprehend that one data is related to another, which may be obvious to us. We will gain exposure to managing data relationships in this recipe.

The following are the steps to manage data relationships by creating a copy of the `DatabaseData_v3.xlsx` file, which results in the creation of the `Relationships` sheet:

1. Make a copy of the `DatabaseData_v3.xlsx` file and save as `DatabaseData_v3_test.xlsx`. Copy the sheet `PivotTable` and rename the sheet as `Relationships`.

2. Firstly, click on the **PowerPivot Window** tab and then under the **Design** tab, click on **Manage Relationships** and remove all relationships. Return to Excel, refresh, and confirm that the results are all out of place as they are not related to one another anymore. Excel will have a **Create** button that says "Relationships may be needed" in the **PowerPivot Field List** dashboard. However, instead of having it automatically generate data, we will manually reproduce it.

3. First, start by studying where the data are. **Number of clients** is from the **BusinessEntityAddress | BusinessEntityID** column, **Country Name** is from the **CountryRegion | Name** column, **State Name** is from **StateProvince | Name**, and **City Name** is from **Address | City**. Then, we can observe that there are common data between the tables, which is how they are linked. The same *key* act as a link in saying that these data are related.

4. Observe the following connections:

   ❑ In the **BusinessEntityAddress** table, there is a single **AddressID** value for each **BusinessEntityID**

   ❑ In the **Address** table, there is a single **City** value and a single **StateProvinceID** value for each **AddressID**

   ❑ In the **StateProvince** table, there is a single **Name** value and a single **CountryRegionCode** value for each **StateProvinceID**

   ❑ In the **CountryRegion** table, there is a single **Name** value for each **CountryRegionCode**

5. As evidenced, one data links to another table, whose value links to another table.

6. Then, create the relationships in the mentioned order. For instance, the first relationship created would be as follows:

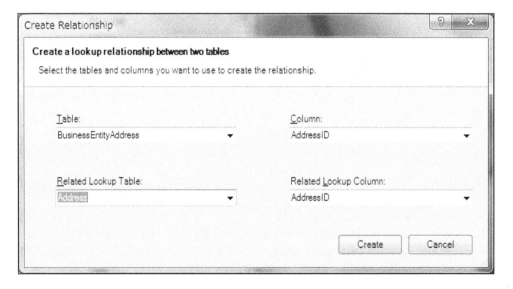

7. After creating the third relationship, return to Excel, refresh, and check the results. Congratulations! We have managed to link all the relevant data together to reproduce our previous settings.

8. Now, create two more relationships:

   ❑ Link **BusinessEntityID** between the tables **BusinessEntityAddress** and **PersonPhone**

   ❑ Link **PhoneNumberTypeID** between the tables **PersonPhone** and **PhoneNumberType**

9. We have successfully linked the phone number of each client, and then linked the phone type of each phone number. Return to Excel, refresh, and add **PhoneNumberType | Name** into **Slicers Horizontal**. The result would appear as shown in the following screenshot:

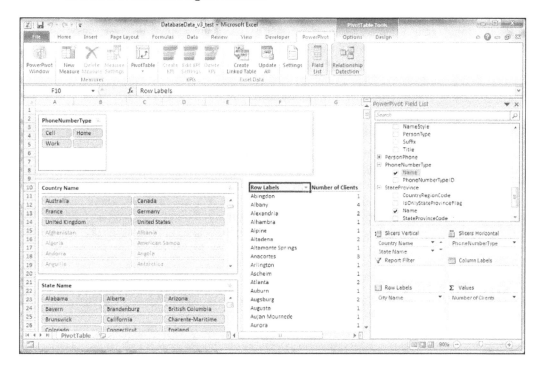

10. We can now sort the clients by their phone number types, and can reach conclusions such as that no one from Australia, France, and Germany has provided their work phone numbers, and that some of the phone numbers are not categorized under **Home**, **Work**, or **Cell**.

11. If we were to produce the same pivot table in the original `DatabaseData_v3.xlsx` file, the phone number types will not show in the pivot table, and PowerPivot will not be able to detect it automatically because its relationship has been set up in another manner.

How it works...

As mentioned, the *Key* acts as a bridge between various tables, enabling PowerPivot to link the data together. In most cases, the auto-detection feature of PowerPivot is sufficient as it auto-detects and utilizes relationships between tables to compile various data together. In this recipe, we have studied the tables independently, analyzed the links between them, and manually reproduced the links between the tables to generate the same pivot table as before by connecting various tables together.

There's more...

There are some tables that cannot be linked despite having links. An example would be using **BusinessEntityID** as a link between **BusinessEntityAddress** and **BusinessEntityContact**. As these tables cannot be linked, the tables linked with **BusinessEntityAddress** (that is, **Address**, **Person**, **EmailAddress**, and **PhoneNumber**) cannot be used in conjunction with the tables linked with **BusinessEntityContact** (that is, **ContactType**).

Creating custom tables instead of connecting relationships

As an alternative to building relationships between various tables, we can just add all the relevant items into one table. This is normally called *View* in a database, where the aggregated data from many tables are shown as a single table. This will be useful for the previously mentioned case, by merging the tables **BusinessEntityAddress** and **BusinessEntityContact** together. We will discuss this method in the following *Adding new custom columns (Intermediate)* recipe, where we learn how to modify PowerPivot data tables using formulas.

Adding new custom columns (Intermediate)

As we saw in previous recipes, sometimes the data by itself is not what we want. Furthermore, we are restricted to what is already available and are unable to arrange the data the way we want it, even if it is rather simple such as arranging it by every five years instead of by every year.

PowerPivot, just like Excel, supports user-friendly manual inputs into data columns, and we are able to input a Data Analysis Expressions (DAX) formula, which is very similar to Excel formulas. By inputting these additional formulas and creating additional columns, we will be able to select from a wider range of data columns to exactly suit our needs.

We will practice various aspects of creating a custom column and the associated benefits by following the steps in this recipe.

Getting ready

To learn the basic formulas of Excel would be beneficial in configuring additional custom data columns.

Then, we will need a new set of data that we can selectively filter, modify, and use. Open up a new instance of PowerPivot and import from SQL. Select all 19 tables that have the **Schema** value as **Sales** and filter out the **Modified Date** and **rowguid** columns in order to be more efficient in storing and calculating the data as shown in the following screenshot:

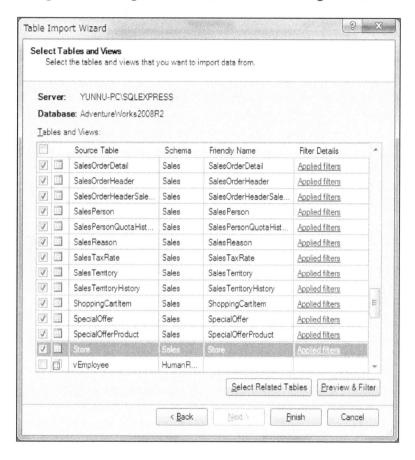

Save the file as `CustomColumns_v1.xlsx`. Refer to the recipe where we imported the data from SQL if we are stuck at any point.

How to do it...

In this section, we will use the imported data and create additional data using custom columns through multiple sheets that build on one another.

The following are the steps to add a new custom column using the `CustomColumns_ v1.xlsx` file, which results in the creation of the `DeliveryTime01` sheet:

1. The table **SalesOrderHeader** contains the **OrderDate**, **DueDate**, **ShipDate**, **OnlineOrderFlag**, **ShipMethodID**, and **TerritoryID** columns. These are the relevant data if we are interested in analyzing the shipping time based on: whether the order was an online order or not, which shipping method was chosen, and which area it was delivered to. We can also analyze whether the shipping period met the due date deadline or not.

2. Create a pivot table in the order you think is necessary to analyze the shipping time for each order. For instance, it would be:

    ❑ Select **SalesOrderHeader | ShipMethodID, SalesOrderHeader | OnlineOrderFlag**, and **SalesTerritory | Name** and move them under **Slicers Vertical**

    ❑ Select **SalesOrderHeader | OrderDate** and move it under **Row Labels**

    ❑ Select **SalesOrderHeader | ShipDate** and **SalesOrderHeader | DueDate** and move them under **Values**

3. However, this does not give us what we want. It only gives us the order date and number of orders that have that order date (**Count of ShipDate** and **Count of DueDate**), which is filterable by the **ShipMethodID** and **OnlineOrderFlag** columns, and the destination region.

4. What we want is the duration it took to ship, and whether it met the due date. Because we can't manually type data inside the pivot table, there is no way to know both of these. This is where it is crucial to add custom columns manually.

5. Return to PowerPivot. Under the **Design** tab, click on the **Add** button to add a new column to calculate the number of days it took to ship from the moment of order. Type in the formula as follows:

    ```
    = [ShipDate] - [OrderDate]
    ```

6. It will create a column called **CalculatedColumn1** showing the bunch of **1900/01/06 0:00:00**. Let us change the format to numbers so that it may represent the number of days between order and shipping as shown. Also, change the name of the column to `ShippingDays`.

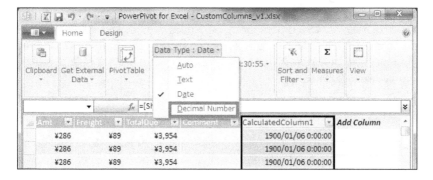

7. Then, because we want to see if it shipped before the due date, create another custom column with the following formula:

```
= [ShipDate] <= [DueDate]
```

8. This column will return a Boolean (**True** or **False**) as to whether the shipped date is equal to or less than (before) the due date. It will return **True** if it was shipped on or before the due date, and will return **False** if it was shipped past the due date. Change the column name to `DeliveredOnTime`.

9. Return to the pivot table and refresh. Remove all three datasets from **Row Labels** and **Values**. Add **ShippingDays** to **Row Labels** and **Slicers Vertical**, add **DeliveredOnTime** to **Slicers Vertical**, and add **SalesOrderID** to **Values** and change it to **Count of SalesOrderID**. The pivot table should appear as follows:

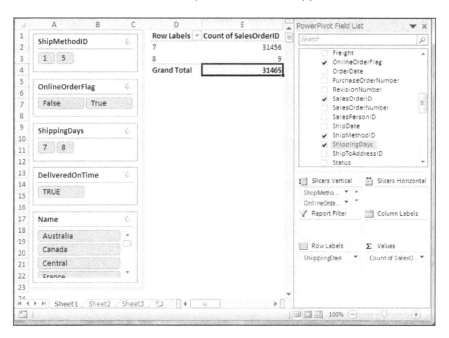

10. Now, we have what we want: number of days it took to ship (**7** or **8**) and number of orders for each (**31456** orders that took **7** days to ship, and **9** orders that took **8** days to ship). By filtering the data using our slicers (**ShipMethodID, OnlineOrderFlag, ShippingDays, DeliveredOnTime**, and **RegionName**), we are able to make a number of conclusions such as:

   □ All orders were shipped on time (**DeliveredOnTime** is **True** for all orders)

   □ All online orders took **7** days to ship (when **OnlineOrderFlag** is True)

   □ All online orders are shipped using ship method ID **1**, and all non-online orders are shipped using ship method ID **5** (when filtering by **OrderOnlineFlag**)

   □ Germany is the only country where some of the orders took **8** days to arrive (when **8** is selected in the **ShippingDays** filter)

11. This is good! We are getting used to modifying the data by adding custom columns to give us what we want—and to make conclusions based on those data.

12. Save the sheet as `DeliveryTime01` and save the file.

The following are the steps to add a new custom column using the `DeliveryTime01` sheet in the `CustomColumns_v1.xlsx` file, which results in the creation of the `DeliveryTime02` sheet:

1. Copy the sheet `DeliveryTime01` and rename as `DeliveryTime02`.

2. Now we want to expand on this to see the per-month, per-season, and per-year result of number of orders. However, a quick look at the PowerPivot table suggests that the closest data we have is the order date column, which gives date format in a number not orderable by year, by season, or by month. Well then, it's time for custom columns.

3. Return to the PowerPivot table **SalesOrderHeader** and add three custom columns with the following formulas and rename them as `Year`, `Month`, and `Season` respectively. It should appear as follows.

   ```
   =year([OrderDate])
   =month([OrderDate])
   =if(or([Month]<3, [Month]=12), "Winter", if([Month]<6, "Spring",
   if([Month]<9, "Summer", "Fall")))
   ```

4. The previous three lines of code are shown in columns **Year, Month**, and **Season** as shown in the following screenshot:

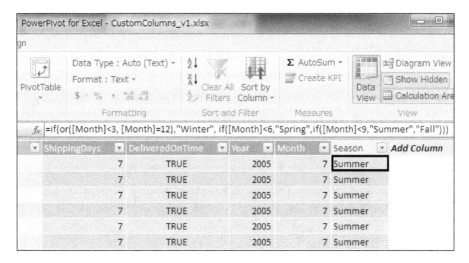

5. Return to the pivot table, and let us reformat the slicers. From **Slicers Vertical**, since all orders were delivered on time, remove **DeliveredOnTime**. Since all online orders are shipped using the ship method ID **1** and all non-online orders are shipped using the ship method ID **5**, remove **ShipMethodID**. Then, in **Slicers Horizontal**, add **Year**, **Month**, and **Season**.

6. Well that was relatively easy, wasn't it?

7. Our analysis shows that the deliveries took longer than usual (**8** days instead of **7**) only during the year of 2008 in February, March, April, and May, for Germany only. We also observe that orders were relatively well distributed over the months as well as the season. The number of orders has been steadily increasing since 2005, so that's good.

8. One thing rather troublesome in our analysis is that the regions of U.S. are treated separately. Let us fix that and have all the U.S. regions as United States. Since the **RegionName** value comes from the table **SalesTerritory**, let's re-open PowerPivot and check the table.

9. Oh! It seems that there is already a column called **CountryRegionCode** that shows the country, instead of the region! Let us use this. Return to the pivot table and replace the filter **Name** with **SalesTerritory | CountryRegionCode**. We have just saved unnecessary work by finding another column that serves our purpose exactly. It is worthwhile to note that the U.S. only accounts for about 40 percent of our sale, meaning that we are a very international company with much room for growth.

10. Let's save the file for now.

The following are the steps to add a new custom column using the `DeliveryTime02` sheet in the `CustomColumns_v1.xlsx` file, which results in the creation of the `DeliveryTime03` sheet:

1. Copy over the `DeliveryTime02` sheet, and rename as `DeliveryTime03`.

2. In treating orders, the number of orders is important. However, what is more important is how much we made from those orders! We want to expand our table even further to see our revenue made from these orders per month. Let us rearrange the data:

   ❑ Remove all datasets from **Row Labels** and **Values**

   ❑ Move all datasets in **Slicers Horizontal** to **Slicers Vertical** (reorder as **Year, Month, Season, CountryRegionCode, OnlineOrderFlag**, and **ShippingDays**)

   ❑ Add **Year** and **Month** to **Row Labels**

   ❑ Add **SubTotal, TaxAmt**, and **Freight**, all as a **Sum**

3. Now we have a per month, per year figure of sales, tax, freight fees, and total charged on orders. An analysis could be made that while the number of orders is relatively stable throughout the year (based on the previous sheets), the amount of an order is generally lower in January and higher during the months of June to August. The absolute $ amount helps us to understand our businesses better.

4. However, the sheer numbers may be difficult to see at times. Create a doughnut-style pivot chart and click on **Switch Row/Column**. As we filter through the data using slicers, the pivot chart makes it easier for us to observe trends. For instance, the tax rates for the United Kingdom and France increased around the middle of 2006; the tax rate for Germany increased around the middle of 2007.

5. We can further modify the data for our analysis by changing the data type from **Sum** to **Count, Min, Max, Average**, and **DistinctCount** as shown in the following screenshot:

6. Each will give a unique result: total order dollar amount, total number of orders, cheapest order, most expensive order, average of order, and number of different amounts of order, all on a monthly basis. Modify the fields as you will and try to comprehend the results.

7. Save the file.

We have practiced creating various custom columns for our analysis. These custom columns are very useful as they allow us to create and store all the relevant data in one table. Let us continue such analysis to a greater extent in the following recipe in a new sheet.

The following are the steps to add a new custom column using the `DeliveryTime03` sheet in the `CustomColumns_v1.xlsx` file, which results in the creation of the `DeliveryTime04` sheet:

1. Copy over the sheet `DeliveryTime03` and rename as `DeliveryTime04`.

2. To further our analysis, we want to look at which product sold well over the years. Looking at the PowerPivot tables, we know that the detail of each order is stored in the **SalesOrderDetail** table, with **ProductID**, **UnitPrice**, **LineTotal**, and so on. Based on our experience so far, it is logical that **ProductID** links the **SalesOrderDetail** table to another **Product** table that we don't have right now; let us import that table as well so that we know which product ID corresponds to which product.

3. Follow the same steps for importing data from the database. Looking through the tables, we find that the table **Product** contains both the **ProductID** and **Name** columns, which states what the product is for each **ProductID**. Since we are only interested in the names of the products, in **Preview & Filter**, deselect all columns and select only the **ProductID** and **Name** columns for import, as shown in the following screenshot:

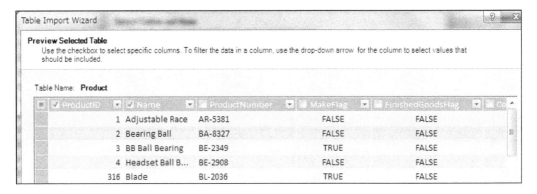

4. Return to the pivot table/chart. Click on the pivot chart and then click on **Switch Row/Column Data** to have the year and months as the rows, and **SubTotal**, **TaxAmt**, and **Freight** as the columns. Then update the **PowerPivot Field List** dashboard as follows:

   ❑ In the **Values** field, delete all (**SubTotal**, **TaxAmt**, and **Freight**), then add **LineTotal** and **OrderQty** from the **SalesOrderDetail** table

   ❑ Add **Product | Name** to **Slicers Horizontal**

   ❑ Click on the **Create** relationships button as requested by PowerPivot

   ❑ Change the formatting of cells to comma style

5. In the pivot table, we now have the number of orders and dollar amount of those orders on a monthly basis, filterable by products, year, month, season, country, online order flag, and shipping days. This data is relatively easy to comprehend based on the pivot table. For instance, we can easily see that the product **All-purpose Bike Stand** was first ordered in July 2007 and has been selling at a rate of roughly 20/month. If we analyze even further, we may be able to find which products are popular for each region.

6. Due to the large number of products, the pivot chart is not useful for this purpose. Similar to **CountryRegionCode**, if we can find some data or create another custom column to sort products by other criteria such as accessories, bike gear, and clothes, then the pivot table may be useful in helping us comprehend the data quicker.

7. Save and close the file.

How it works...

Throughout the four sheets, we have combined everything that we have learned so far to analyze various types of results using PowerPivot. With the addition of custom columns, there is no limit or boundary on what kind of business intelligence analysis we could perform.

In the first sheet (`DeliveryTime01`), we have put together everything we have learned in previous recipes, and learned the methods behind creating custom columns. We used the custom column generated data in the pivot table to give us the filters we want in the format we want.

The first formula we used (`= [ShipDate] - [OrderDate]`) simply subtracts the order date from the ship date, giving us 0 if shipped on the same day, 1 if shipped the next day, and so on.

Similarly, the second formula used (`= [ShipDate] <= [DueDate]`) returns `TRUE` if the due date is equal to or greater than the ship date (shipped before the due date), and returns `FALSE` if shipped after the due date.

We then rearranged the slicers and values to make a set of conclusions, which are evident simply by changing various slicer settings.

In the second sheet (`DeliveryTime02`), we further practiced creating custom columns with more advanced and frequently used Excel formulas for date analysis. The first two formulas (year and month) are rather self-explanatory in that they simply return the year/month of the date given. The last formula for season is slightly more complicated. Let us have a look:

```
=if(or([Month]<3, [Month]=12), "Winter", if([Month]<6, "Spring",
if([Month]<9, "Summer", "Fall")))
```

This can be rearranged as follows:

```
=if(or([Month]<3, [Month]=12), "Winter",
   if([Month]<6, "Spring",
      if([Month]<9, "Summer",
         "Fall")))
```

The first part checks if the month is less than 3, or is equal to 12, (that is, it checks if the month is 1, 2, or 12) and returns `Winter` if true, and moves on to the next statement if false. The second line performs a similar check—if the month is less than 6 (that is, if the month is equal to 3 or 4 or 5), it will return `Spring` and otherwise move on to the next line.

You may wonder why it does not return 1, 2, 3, 4, or 5, when the formula clearly says less than 6 (<6). This is because the second line is only used when the first line is false, and the first line is false if the month is not 1, 2, or 12. Thus, the second line only checks if the month is equal to 3, 4, or 5.

The third line is similar in format. It will return `Summer` if less than 9 (or equal to 6, 7, or 8), and return `Fall` otherwise (is equal to 9, 10, or 11).

We then rearranged our **PowerPivot Field List** dashboard further and made further analysis. We also changed which data column we were using instead of manually creating another custom column to aggregate regions by country. This is the smarter choice as there is no need to reinvent the wheel.

In the third sheet (`DeliveryTime03`), we expanded our analysis to include dollar amounts instead of just the number of orders. After all of our practice, this was a rather easy step that just required us to analyze which table/column is relevant, and how to combine them in the pivot table.

We created a further pivot chart and switched rows/columns to view our data more easily, as the percentage value is easier to compare than absolute values. We also learned that we can come up with a totally different set of data values by simply changing how the data is summarized.

In the last sheet (`DeliveryTime04`), we moved away from the data we were using, and used data columns from another table and imported a new table from the database for our purpose as well. We gave the pivot table a new slicer to filter by products.

In total, we have moved on from a simple date analysis to quantity analysis, then to revenue analysis and extended-revenue analysis. All of this was done by selecting data, using slicers, and adding custom columns appropriately. There is no limit to what kind of analysis could be performed by using these methods, in combination with a pivot table and a pivot chart, to display the data in an intelligent manner that may be easily interpreted.

There's more...

At any time, if PowerPivot does not refresh properly into Excel, restart Excel.

Refer to Excel's built-in formula helper (the **Insert Function** button) to type in what you need, and use the same formula in creating new custom columns.

Making the data look presentable (Simple)

We've put data in a pivot table and a pivot chart to make them comprehensible and easy-to-find trends. However, that is not enough. The easier it is to see the trends, the more effective the work is; and just like how famous brands use marketing to their advantage, we are going to package our little product to make it more appealing, more meaningful.

We will focus on features outside of pivot tables and pivot charts since there are millions of ways to represent the data in those two. Instead, we will build upon what we have prepared so far to redesign, organize, and clean up our data.

Getting ready

From the previous recipe, prepare the file `CustomColumns_v1.xlsx`. Open it up, copy the sheet `DeliveryTime04`, and save the copied sheet as `Result`.

How to do it...

1. Can we present this to our boss? No, of course not. The pivot chart does not mean anything, there is a field called **Row Labels**, and it just does not look presentable in any way or form. This is no different than just providing the raw database's data and telling someone to interpret it, not to our standard.

2. Then let's start re-packaging our results. Firstly, let us name items by changing the **Row Labels** value to `Year/Month` as shown in the following screenshot:

Row Labels ▼	Sum of OrderQty	Sum of LineTotal
⊟ 2005	11,848	11,331,809
7	966	962,717
8	2,209	2,044,600
9	1,658	1,639,840
10	1,403	1,358,050
11	3,132	2,868,129
12	2,480	2,458,472
⊟ 2006	60,918	30,674,773

3. Then, also change the names of slicers as follows:

   ❑ Change **CountryRegionCode** to `Country Name`

   ❑ Change **OnlineOrderFlag** to `Online Order?`

   ❑ Change **ShippingDays** to `Shipment Duration (days)`

   ❑ Change **Name** to `Product Name`

   ❑ Move all vertical slicers to horizontal

4. Click on the pivot chart. Under the **Design** tab, click on **Switch Row/Column**. Now our pivot table will be represented horizontally. However, this is too long! Move the **Year** dataset from **Column Labels** to **Row Labels**.

5. Oh! As we have changed our row, **Row Labels** and **Column Labels** appeared again. Rename as `Year` and `Month` respectively. Also change the **Sum of OrderQty** and **Sum of LineTotal** options to `Order Quantity` and `Order Amount ($)` respectively.

6. Create an additional pivot chart (copy over the previous one). Set the first chart type as doughnut, and the second chart type as bar graph. Place underneath the pivot table.

7. Above the pivot table, extend the horizontal slicers to match the size of the pivot table as well. Rearrange as necessary. It may sound feasible to remove the **Month** slicer because we can easily compare the monthly results year over year, but we will not remove it because it helps us to filter our graphs, which would otherwise show all 12 months at the same time.

8. Since we can see the direct numbers from the pivot table, we don't need exact numbers in the pivot charts. Instead, the pivot chart should be used to observe trends. Thus, we will modify our bar graph, which doesn't show us much information other than the **Order Amount ($)** values due to the sheer largeness of the order amount in comparison to the order quantity.

9. Double-click on vertical axis, and under **Axis Options**, check the **Logarithmic Scale** option. Then manually specify the **Minimum** value as `100`. Now we have represented the values in logs of 10. The result should be as shown in the following screenshot:

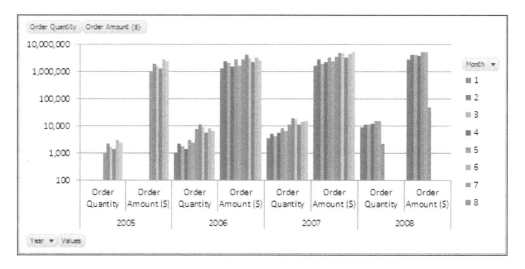

10. Even though we may not have specific values, it is so much easier to observe the trends—whether the sales have increased or decreased over the months. We are able to observe in more detail if we use the horizontal slicers to filter using per product, or per year. And if we need specific figures, we can always refer to the preceding pivot table.

11. For instance, by filtering on yearly basis, we can clearly observe that the increase in number of products sold signifies greater sales revenue. Although it may sound obvious that the more products we sell, the more money we make, it is not necessarily the case as 2007 December appears to have sold fewer products than 2007 August, but has higher revenue ($ amount sold). Referring to the pivot table, we can observe that it is indeed true: December sold about 3,000 fewer products, but generated about $200,000 more than August.

12. We also notice in the bar graph that the online orders have increased sharply in the middle of 2007, and that orders have been increasing ever since. By filtering based on **Months**, the doughnut graph makes it easy to view year-over-year changes in the orders.

13. We can filter through more, but the format is not good as the pivot table seems to resize based on which slicers we use. Rearrange the orders to slicers, pivot charts, and then pivot tables. The slicer also has many criteria, and we can remove the overlapping ones. In this case, that would be the seasons, as we can manually filter by selecting the months, instead of the seasons (that is, clicking on **1**, **2**, and **12** using the **Month** slicer will give the same result as clicking on the **Winter** slicer). Thus, remove the **Seasons** filter.

14. Also remove **Shipment Duration (days)** as we are not interested anymore in few outliers, which took one day more to ship. That leaves more space for the **Product Name** slicer, enabling us to scroll through faster.

15. Now, since our pivot table, chart, and slicers look good, it's time to make the final arrangements using Excel.

16. Under the third tab, **Page Layout**, uncheck the **View** button of the **Gridlines** button. It removed all gridlines in the background, making it look more clean and crisp. Also change the color of the sheet to red, highlighting that this is the final, most relevant sheet. The final product should appear as shown in the following screenshot:

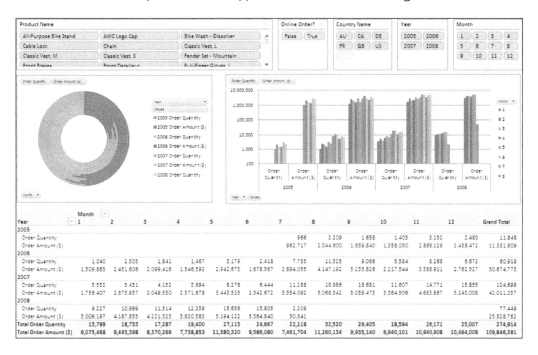

Year	Month												Grand Total
	1	2	3	4	5	6	7	8	9	10	11	12	
2005													
Order Quantity							966	2,209	1,658	1,403	3,132	2,480	11,848
Order Amount ($)							962,717	2,044,600	1,639,840	1,358,090	2,868,129	2,458,472	11,331,809
2006													
Order Quantity	1,040	2,303	1,841	1,467	3,179	2,418	7,755	11,325	9,066	5,584	8,268	6,672	60,918
Order Amount ($)	1,309,863	2,451,606	2,099,416	1,546,592	2,942,673	1,678,567	2,894,055	4,147,192	3,235,826	2,217,544	3,388,911	2,762,527	30,674,773
2007													
Order Quantity	3,532	5,431	4,132	5,694	8,278	6,444	11,288	18,986	18,681	11,607	14,771	15,855	124,699
Order Amount ($)	1,756,407	2,873,937	2,049,530	2,571,678	3,448,525	2,542,672	3,554,092	5,068,342	5,059,473	3,564,506	4,683,867	5,243,008	42,011,037
2008													
Order Quantity	9,227	10,999	11,314	12,239	15,656	15,805	2,209						77,449
Order Amount ($)	3,009,197	4,167,855	4,221,323	3,820,583	5,194,122	5,364,840	50,841						25,828,762
Total Order Quantity	13,799	18,733	17,287	19,400	27,113	24,667	22,218	32,520	29,405	18,594	26,171	25,007	274,914
Total Order Amount ($)	6,075,468	9,493,398	8,370,269	7,738,853	11,580,320	9,586,080	7,461,704	11,260,134	9,935,140	6,940,101	10,940,908	10,464,008	109,846,381

17. In short, the final preparation step for creating a presentation-worthy PowerPivot is as follows:

    ❑ Rearrange all data such that the graphs and/or tables are not too wide or long, so that a glance should provide some understanding of the material

    ❑ Rename all filters, tables, and charts so that anyone who is somewhat familiar with the material is able to comprehend at once what each items are

    ❑ Perform typical Excel steps in creating an overview/result/summary sheet by removing backgrounds, highlighting sheets, and saving the file with a proper naming convention

How it works...

We are done in preparing our file! The final product appears comprehensive, understandable, and presents both graphs for trends and table for actual figures. The background is clean, white space, the figures change based on our slicers, and we are able to make an analysis on it, and are able to send it to others to share our results!

We have managed to achieve this by rearranging, reconfiguring our data, renaming, and adding/removing items and backgrounds to make it look more appealing in both a data-analytical sense and in an aesthetical sense.

There's more...

There are resources online on making your Excel appear more professional. Since PowerPivot builds upon Excel 2010, it may be of use to look these tips up online since an Excel file can never look *too good*.

Publishing as Excel (Simple)

One may wonder why there is a recipe on publishing as Excel as the file is already in Excel 2010 format. That is because in typical workplaces without SharePoint server, there are limits to e-mail attachments and inboxes, and sharing large files that we have conducted our analysis on becomes much more difficult. In this recipe, we will practice how to identify irrelevant data and how to remove them from our file for efficiency.

Getting ready

Copy over the file `CustomColumns_v1.xlsx` and renamed the copied file as `AdventureWorks Order Quantity and Revenue Analysis_v1.xlsx`. The former file should be about 11.2 MB in size.

How to do it...

1. First, since all our data is stored in PowerPivot and not in other sheets, we can simply remove all sheets except the final sheet **Result**. This alone should save about 0.1 MB.

2. Then, going through all the data tables we have as shown under the **PowerPivot Field List** dashboard, we notice many of the data tables are not used at all. For instance, the table **CreditCard** contains none of the information we are using nor contains any significant relationships that we should not remove in order to maintain our data's sanity. Then, logically, let's delete the table.

3. Open up PowerPivot. We notice sheets such as **CreditCard** contains about 19,000 rows. Let's delete the whole table by right-clicking on the sheet name and selecting **Delete**. Luckily for us, the data used in our analysis came from few major tables only so we probably will not make a mistake of removing a crucial table by accident.

4. Delete all data tables (sheets) except for **SalesOrderHeader**, **SalesOrderDetail**, **SalesReason**, **SalesTerritory**, and **Product**. If you are unsure at any point whether the table is used, the simplest way to check is to go back to the pivot table/chart and see which fields are being used (checked) under the **PowerPivot Field List** dashboard. The file should be about 7.0 MB after deletion.

5. Even though we managed to delete the unused data tables, the file is still very large for such a basic analysis. If we were to perform a more extensive analysis, no doubt the file will be tens of megabytes. Thus, we will optimize our file further by removing unused columns as well, just like how we had filtered out the date log column when we first imported the data.

6. In the table **SalesOrderHeader**, remove the following columns: **Revision**, **Status**, **SalesOrderNumber**, **PurchaseOrderNumber**, **AccountNumber**, **CustomerID**, **SalesPersonID**, **BilltoAddressID**, **ShipToAddressID**, **CreditCardID**, **CreditCardApprovalCode**, and **CurrencyRateID**. This saves an additional 2.6 MB, for a file size of 4.4 MB.

7. In the table **SalesOrderDetail**, remove the following columns: **SalesOrderDetailID** and **CarrierTrackingNumber**. This saves an additional 1.8 MB, for a file size of 2.6 MB.

8. This is good. We have managed to still maintain all critical data used in our analysis and have shrunk the file size to about 25 percent of the original by simply removing unused tables and columns. 2.5 MB is small enough to be sent over e-mail easily! Save as Excel and close. It will be readable by anyone with access to Excel 2010.

How it works...

Similar to filtering out tables and columns during the data export, we have simply removed unnecessary columns and kept the critical columns as well as a few more columns that may be useful for further analysis.

It is important to note that deleting a column from a table with 100,000 rows is more effective in reducing the file size than deleting 5 columns from a table with 18,000 rows. Such was the case in our file where we deleted 12 columns in **SalesOrderHeader**, which has 31,465 rows (a total of roughly 360,000 cells deleted), while simply deleting two columns from **SalesOrderDetail**, which has 121,317 rows (a total of roughly 240,000 rows deleted) reduced the file size in a similar manner.

There's more...

If PowerPivot contains a data table that is not used now but may be used in the future, then we can simply hide the sheet by right-clicking on the sheet and selecting **Hide from Client Tools** instead of deleting the sheet and re-importing it later on.

Version compatibility issue

With the new Excel 2013, there is now a version compatibility issue between Excel files created with different PowerPivot versions. This further complicates things, especially if the business uses SharePoint servers, as they require the same PowerPivot version installed and configured or otherwise they will encounter errors.

In short, like all programs with different versions, Excel files created with the older version of PowerPivot will be accessible in the newer version, but the Excel file created with newer versions of PowerPivot will not be accessible with an older version of PowerPivot.

For more details, please refer to resources such as:

- ► `http://office.microsoft.com/en-us/excel-help/version-compatibility-between-powerpivot-data-models-in-excel-2010-and-excel-2013-HA103929426.aspx`
- ► `http://technet.microsoft.com/en-us/library/jj219751.aspx`
- ► `http://sqlblog.com/blogs/marco_russo/archive/2013/01/14/powerpivot-compatibility-across-versions.aspx`

Thank you for buying
Instant Creating Data Models with PowerPivot How-to

About Packt Publishing

Packt, pronounced 'packed', published its first book "*Mastering phpMyAdmin for Effective MySQL Management*" in April 2004 and subsequently continued to specialize in publishing highly focused books on specific technologies and solutions.

Our books and publications share the experiences of your fellow IT professionals in adapting and customizing today's systems, applications, and frameworks. Our solution based books give you the knowledge and power to customize the software and technologies you're using to get the job done. Packt books are more specific and less general than the IT books you have seen in the past. Our unique business model allows us to bring you more focused information, giving you more of what you need to know, and less of what you don't.

Packt is a modern, yet unique publishing company, which focuses on producing quality, cutting-edge books for communities of developers, administrators, and newbies alike. For more information, please visit our website: www.packtpub.com.

Writing for Packt

We welcome all inquiries from people who are interested in authoring. Book proposals should be sent to author@packtpub.com. If your book idea is still at an early stage and you would like to discuss it first before writing a formal book proposal, contact us; one of our commissioning editors will get in touch with you.

We're not just looking for published authors; if you have strong technical skills but no writing experience, our experienced editors can help you develop a writing career, or simply get some additional reward for your expertise.

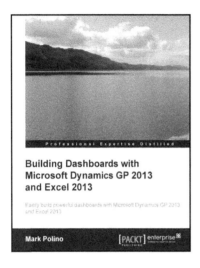

Building Dashboards with Microsoft Dynamics GP 2013 and Excel 2013

Building Dashboards with
Microsoft Dynamics GP 2013
and Excel 2013

Easily build powerful dashboards with Microsoft Dynamics GP 2013
and Excel 2013

Mark Polino

Building Dashboards with Microsoft Dynamics GP 2013 and Excel 2013

ISBN: 978-1-84968-906-9   Paperback: 268 pages

Easily build powerful dashboards with Microsoft Dynamics GP 2013 and Excel 2013

1. Build a dashboard using Excel 2013 with information from Microsoft Dynamics GP 2013

2. Make Excel a true business intelligence tool with charts, sparklines, slicers, and more

3. Utilize PowerPivot's full potential to create even more complex dashboards

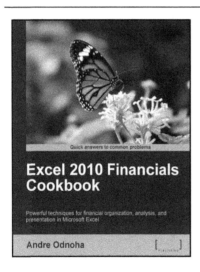

Excel 2010 Financials Cookbook

Powerful techniques for financial organization, analysis, and presentation in Microsoft Excel

Andre Odnoha

Excel 2010 Financials Cookbook

ISBN: 978-1-84969-118-5   Paperback: 260 pages

Powerful techniques for financial organization, analysis, and presentation in Microsoft Excel

1. Harness the power of Excel to help manage your business finances

2. Build useful financial analysis systems on top of Excel

3. Covers normalizing, analysing, and presenting financial data

4. Clear and practical with straight forward, step-by-step instructions

Please check **www.PacktPub.com** for information on our titles

PUBLISHING

Microsoft Dynamics CRM 2011:
Dashboards Cookbook

Over 50 simple but incredibly effective recipes for creating,
customizing and interacting with rich dashboards and charts

Mark AuCoin

Microsoft Dynamics CRM 2011: Dashboards Cookbook

ISBN: 978-1-84968-440-8   Paperback: 266 pages

Over 50 simple but incredibly effective recipes
for creating, customizing and interacting with rich
dashboards and charts

1. Take advantage of all of the latest Dynamics CRM
    dashboard features for visualizing your most
    important data at a glance.

2. Understand how iFrames, chart customizations,
    advanced WebResources and more can improve
    your dashboards in Dynamics CRM by using this
    book and eBook.

Business Intelligence Cookbook:
A Project Lifecycle Approach
Using Oracle Technology

John Heaton

Business Intelligence Cookbook: A Project Lifecycle Approach Using Oracle Technology

ISBN: 978-1-84968-548-1   Paperback: 368 pages

Over 80 quick and advanced recipes that focus on
real-world techniques and solutions to manage, design,
and build data warehouse and business intelligence
projects

1. Full of illustrations, diagrams, and tips with clear
    step-by-step instructions and real time examples
    to perform key steps and functions on your project

2. Practical ways to estimate the effort of a data
    warehouse solution based on a standard work
    breakdown structure.

3. Learn to effectively turn the project from
    development to a live solution

Please check **www.PacktPub.com** for information on our titles